BEST
Pocket Parks
of
NYC

By Rosemary O'Brien

DEDICATION

To Alan, Nicholas and Alexander for all of your love and support while I researched this project and wrote this first guide.

WHY THIS GUIDE?

When I lived and worked in New York City as a young actress, I was always amazed by these little sanctuaries right in the middle of all of the high-rise buildings. They were great places to stop and hang out for someone with little money and time to kill between auditions. This guide covers not only where the best parks are located, but if there is an interesting story, why they were created. When someone needs a place to stop and rest while working in or visiting the City, they can pull out the guide or the website and find a pocket park nearby.

Only the best parks and some public spaces are included here and no one can pay to be included. Of course, 'best' is defined by me at the moment. If you think there is a park or public space that should be included, please go to my website at http://www.PocketParksNYC.com, fill out the comment form and tell me about it. Be sure to include the location. Keep in mind that it was probably excluded intentionally, but I am happy to investigate and may consider adding it to the next edition.

I have taken the liberty to include some of the locations on the New York City Department of Parks and Recreations list of parks. While they are not privately-owned like most of the parks represented in this guide, they were lovely spaces I had to present to my readers. My goal is to give adventurous travelers an appreciation of these little green spaces in the middle of the big city.

I hope you enjoy this guide and the future guides to other cities that are in development.

HISTORY

The 1961 Resolution offered incentives to developers to create public space in exchange for zoning variances for their building projects. In 1965, Mayoral candidate, John Lindsay, took up the gauntlet and he and a number of like-minded citizens decided to spruce up the city a bit. He suggested that New York City create "vest pocket parks" or "adventure playgrounds" from unused plots of land that would otherwise lie fallow. Later, when he was elected Mayor of New York City, he implemented his ideas and helped create the first vest pocket parks in the city. According to an essay on the New York City Department of Parks and Recreation's website, Park Commissioner, Thomas P.F. Hoving encouraged their use for public events and aided Lindsay by bringing various events to the parks. The mayor even went so far as to ban cars in Central Park on Sundays. In 1967, the City completed 10 vest pocket parks in vacant city lots equal to or smaller than one-quarter acre.

Since then, approximately 520 Privately Owned Public Spaces (POPS) have been developed, but many of those spaces are nothing more than widened sidewalks or open plazas. This guide covers those POPS that are welcoming to travelers with adequate and comfortable seating, greenery to mask the hustle and bustle of the city a bit, and aesthetic amenities such as sculptures, or water events such as fountains or gazing pools. It also includes a few that are not officially considered POPS, but are interesting and comfortable places to visit.

I hope readers find this guide helpful and welcome any and all suggestions.

ACKNOWLEDGEMENTS

I would like to take a moment to acknowledge those who have helped get this first guide off the ground. Thank you go out to Jerold S. Kayden, the author of "Privately Owned Public Space: The New York City Experience" along with the New York City Department of City Planning and the Municipal Arts Society for initially documenting all of the POPS in New York City and creating a database with all of their locations. Through this work, these groups and individuals have helped bring these gems to the attention of design students, urban planners and adventurous travelers everywhere.

A very big thank you goes out to the EBV-F (Entrepreneurial Bootcamp for Veterans' Families) at Florida State University for always having my back. What began as one book has turned into several books through their training and generous assistance.

To my intern, Jessica Venables, for helping me through her insight and excellent research skills.

To Mario Burger of Burger International Photography for the use of his photos of POPS throughout the book.

To Nicholas Alfonso for helping me photograph some of the parks and providing a fun day of site visits.

Most of all I would like to thank my husband and sons for putting up with my long hours while I visited sites, researched and spent many hours away from them. Thank you with all of my heart.

REVEREND LINNETTE C. WILLIAMSON
MEMORIAL PARK

Courtesy Reverend Linnette C. Williamson Memorial Park Foundation

65 WEST 128TH STREET

The very first pocket park was created in an empty lot at 65 West 128th by students from the School of Architecture at Columbia University. The Park Association of New York City, now known as New Yorkers for Parks, took up the call under the leadership of Whitney North Seymour, Jr.

Mr. Seymour was instrumental in bringing together philanthropists and community leaders in response to Thomas P.F. Hoving's call for open-space and green areas for the areas of the city most in need. Hoving later became New York City's first Parks Commissioner under Mayor John Lindsay. Reverend Linnette C. Williamson of Christ Community Church of Harlem offered the space next to her church as the first to be developed and it was dedicated in her honor.

Designed by School of Architecture, Columbia University
Completed 1965 (Renovated 1994 by The Park Association)

PALEY PARK

3 EAST 53RD STREET

Paley Park, and its sister park, Greenacre Park, is a perfect example of what a pocket park should be according to the Project for Public Spaces. It sits right in the middle of the city and provides a welcome respite from the hustle and bustle. Created by Zion and Breene Associates for the William S. Paley Foundation, this 4200 square foot space was named in honor of Samuel Paley, William S. Paley's father. William participated in every aspect of its development. It contains 17 honey locust trees, lush, green ivy, and ample tables and chairs. One of its best features is the 20-foot waterfall which uses 1800 gallon per minute. The white noise it creates as it cascades onto the rocks below masks the city noises and evokes peace in an otherwise chaotic city.

Designed by Zion and Breene Associates
Completed 1967

GREENACRE PARK

217 EAST 51ST STREET

Greenacre Park on East 51st Street between Second and Third Avenues is, as mentioned earlier, Paley Park's sister park. Neither are on the city's database of Privately Owned Public Spaces (POPS), but they warrant mention due to their popularity and style.

According to a variety of groups including the Project for Public Space, both Greenacre and Paley Park have all of the basic components that make up a good public space. They are easy to access, contain ample movable seating, have a focal point such as a waterfall to mask street noise while also making a dramatic effect and the there is enough shade to make it a comfortable place to stop during busy city travels.

Designed by Hideo Sasaki and Harmon Goldstone
Completed 1971

QUEEN ELIZABETH II SEPTEMBER 11TH
GARDEN AT HANOVER SQUARE

© 2014 Mario Burger, Burger International Photography

PEARL STREET BETWEEN HANOVER
AND WILLIAMS STREETS

Hanover Square has been in continuous use since 1637 and received its name by 1730. The name was derived from King George I who was from the House of Hanover and this square was a tribute to him. In 2009, a garden was constructed and christened by Prince Harry of Wales as The British Garden at Hanover Square. Rededicated in 2012 as The Queen Elizabeth II September 11th Garden, it now commemorates the British victims of the 9/11 attacks and also acts as a ceremonial space for British ceremonies and functions. Since New Yorkers are slow to call an established location by a new name, it will probably continue to be called The British Garden or simply Hanover Square.

Designed by: Emery Roth & Sons (square) and Julian and Isabel Bannerman (garden)
Completed 1983 (square) and 2009 (garden)

ELEVATED ACRE

© 2014 Mario Burger, Burger International Photography

55 WATER STREET

55 Water Street, better known as the Elevated Acre, has undergone a transformation since it was first developed in 1970. Back then, it was poorly planned and relatively unused. Part of the problem may have been due to its relative seclusion. While it is still out of the way and you really have to look for it, Goldman Sachs and the Municipal Arts Society had it renovated in 2005 and now it is a sunny, inviting space with excellent views of the Financial District and the East River not to mention the outdoor movie events frequently held on the plaza. Located three stories above Water Street, it is one of only six elevated outdoor spaces in Manhattan according to Jerold Kayden.

Designed by Ken Smith and Rogers/Marvel
Completed 2005

BENNETT PARK

© 2014 Nicholas Alfonso

77 WATER STREET

Bennett Park is a plaza on the Gouverneur Lane side of 77 Water Street. There is built-in bench seating, some trees and greenery, and sometimes shade when the sun hits it correctly. An inviting plaza filled with whimsical art and sculpture, you almost forget to look at the building because of it.

The eye is immediately drawn to *Helix* (1969), a sculpture by Rudolph de Harak. Harak took 120 one-inch thick stainless steel strips to create a spiral that looks like a helix or a strand of DNA. *Cityscape Fountains* (1969) is no longer there, but its shell remains. *Rejected Skin* (1969) by William Tarr consists of two blocks of metal created from aluminum panels rejected from the construction of 77 Water Street which sit below a metal cube suspended in mid-air. Behind is an installation called *Month of June* by George Adamy. These variously-colored disks stand upright on white circular pads below.

Designed by Emery Roth & Sons
Completed 1970

111 WALL STREET

© 2014 Nicholas Alfonso

111 WALL STREET

111 Wall Street takes up an entire city block bordered by Front Street, Gouverneur Lane, South Street and Wall Street. There are three very comfortable spaces to sit and relax. The space on Gouverneur Lane is my favorite at this address because the trees are lush enough to provide shade in an area where it can get pretty hot and humid in the summer. If you like the sun, however, you will find the stationary benches on Front Street a great place to sit while you have lunch and people watch.

Designed by Emery Roth & Sons; Thomas Balsley Associates (for alteration)
Completed 1967

BARCLAYS BANK

© 2014 Nicholas Alfonso

75 WALL STREET

The Barclay's Bank space at 75 Wall Street has a lovely rectangular urban plaza at its back that acts as a pass-through between Pearl Street and Water Street. Though its address is Wall Street, the entrance to the plaza on Water Street is the nicest, sporting a banner announcing the Andaz Farmer's Market. In summer months, the market is in full swing on Wednesdays and Saturdays, offering fruits and vegetables from area farmers and food producers. This is touted as the first farmer's market hosted by a New York City hotel, the Andaz Wall Street Hotel, part of the Hyatt Hotels Corporation.

Designed by Welton Becket Associates; M. Paul Friedberg & Partners
Completed 1987

100 WALL STREET

100 WALL STREET

100 Wall Street has a number of stationary benches made of both polished stone and wood. It feels like an extension of the public space just east of it at 110 Wall Street if you look toward the FDR Drive and the East River. Though not technically part of the public space outside, go into the building's lobby and check out the sculpture created by Harold Castor. It depicts events related to General Washington's entrance into New York City. This building has a culture of giving. Savanna, a prominent real estate investment firm in the city, regularly donates space to the Lower Manhattan Culture Council for a residency program which provides exhibition and workspace to artists on an application basis.

Designed by Emery Roth & Sons
Completed 1969

WALL STREET PLAZA

© 2014 Mario Burger, Burger International Photography

88 PINE STREET

Wall Street Plaza is an L-shaped plaza located on Pine Street between Front Street and Water Street The longer part of the L sits on Water Street and hosts a two-piece untitled abstract sculpture created by Yu Yu Yang, a prolific sculptor, environmental designer and architect from Taiwan. The sculpture is a 16-foot-tall rectangle made of steel with a hole cut into the center. The space also sports a memorial to the Queen Elizabeth I, the ship that sank in Hong Kong in 1972 after having caught fire. There is a bronze Q and E taken from the bow, a letter from Queen Elizabeth's private secretary and a telegram from Kurt Waldheim, the former UN Secretary General who hid his Nazi past until his death in 2007.

On the Front Street side, you will come upon a slanted brick wall whose waterfall blocks the sounds of street traffic, and if you look up, you will see owls on the second and third floors of the 88 Pine Street building. No one else looks up, so give them the attention they crave!

Designed by I.M. Pei and Partners;
C.Y. Tung/Morley Cho
Completed 1971

180 MAIDEN LANE

© 2014 Nicholas Alfonso

180 MAIDEN LANE

This amazing outdoor space with a multistory indoor atrium two blocks south of South Street Seaport is as calming as it is spectacular. Encompassing an entire block, 180 Maiden Lane is bordered by Maiden Lane, Front Street, Pine Street and South Street. Outdoors has several stationary benches in interesting patterns under shady trees.

When you enter the indoor atrium, you are surrounded by glass walls that let in tons of light making the space look even larger. The imposing columns seem to be made of brass, but they are actually painted wood in a style known as 'trompe l'oeil,' French for 'deceive the eye.' Several mature trees and ample seating, not to mention the food kiosks, an art exhibition area and public restrooms make this a comfortable place to stop if you are looking to head indoors.

Designed by Swanke Hayden Connell;
Kohn Pedersen Fox; Thomas Balsley
Associates (for Outdoor Public Space).
Completed 1982

60 WALL STREET

© 2014 Nicholas Alfonso

60 WALL STREET

This indoor covered pedestrian space is large, opulent and only one of two fully-enclosed indoor spaces in Lower Manhattan, the other being 180 Maiden Lane. It can be entered on either Wall Street or Pine Street because it passes through halfway between William Street and Pearl Street. All floors have been occupied by Deutsche Bank since their other building was lost during the September 11th attacks.

Movable tables, chairs and a variety of food options line the perimeter of this space which features an escalator to the 2 and 3 subway lines. It was the primary meeting place for organizers during the 'Occupy Wall Street' protests.

Designed by Kevin Roche John Dinkeloo
and Associates
Completed 1989

ZUCCOTTI PARK

© 2014 Nicholas Alfonso

1 LIBERTY PLAZA

Zuccotti Park, a square bordered by Broadway, Trinity Place, Liberty Street and Cedar Street, was formerly known as Liberty Plaza Park before it was damaged during the September 11th attacks on the World Trade Center. They cleaned up the debris and it became a staging area during the recovery efforts. It was renamed after John Zuccotti, the chairman of Brookfield Office Properties at the time the company completed renovations in 2006. In recent history it was the base of the Occupy Wall Street demonstrations.

Zuccotti Park has seating and tables, and briefly featured the World Trade Center Cross before it was moved to the permanent 9/11 Memorial. It hosts two sculptures: Mark Di Suvero's *Joie de Vivre*, and *Double Check* by John Seward Johnson, which is a sculpture of a businessman getting ready to start his day. In the initial hours of the 9/11 attacks, people rushed to the statue thinking it was a man covered in debris and needing aid.

Designed by Cooper, Robertson and Partners
Completed 1968 (renovated 2006)

TRIBECA TOWER

105 DUANE STREET

Tribeca Tower is a residential plaza between Broadway and Church Street, just to the West of 105 Duane Street, its host building. The small trees do nothing to shade the space when the sun is blazing, so it can get rather hot. Metal seating is set into the brick walls which also provide ledge seating and there is a drinking fountain toward the back of the space as well. If you want a sunny space to catch some rays while you grab a bite from one of the nearby food trucks, this space is recommended. Keep in mind that the FDNY is directly across the street, so if they go on a call, it can get noisy.

Designed by Thomas Balsley Associates
Completed 1989

KIMLAU ARCH IN CHATHAM SQUARE

© 2014 Nicholas Alfonso

23 CHATHAM SQUARE

Chatham Square, located at the intersection of Worth Street, St. James Place, Oliver Street and Park Row, is an interesting place to stop. It was named for William Pitt (1708-1778), the First Earl of Chatham and Prime Minister of Great Britain who steadfastly supported a compromise with America as it headed toward war with England in America's War of Independence. It was previously the site of both the Second and Third Avenue Elevated Lines until they were demolished in the mid-20th century. The Second Avenue Subway line is under construction at the site.

The square is home to the Benjamin Ralph Kimlau Memorial Gate, or Kimlau Memorial Arch, named after Lt. Benjamin Ralph Kimlau, a World War II hero of Chinese decent. The American Legion Chinese Memorial Post 1291 which bears his name erected the monument in Lt. Kimlau's honor in 1962. The gate is inscribed in both English and Chinese characters: In memory of the Americans of Chinese ancestry who lost their lives in defense of freedom and democracy.

Designed by architect Poy G. Lee
Completed 1961

THE HILARY GARDENS

© 2014 Mario Burger, Burger International Photography

300 MERCER STREET

This L-shaped space at the base of the Hilary Gardens Apartments at the corner of Mercer and Waverly Place is sunny and entered either from Mercer Street where the building entrance is located or through the open gate on the Waverly Place side. Yes, there is a gate, but since this is a space that is required to be open 24 hours a day, this gate is almost always open.

300 Mercer Street has a number of circular built-in benches which are surrounded by low ledges, in the interior and at the perimeter. This is a nice place to sit when the sun is shining and the fountain is on, though it was off during my last visit. The large fountain is located on the south side of the square.

Designed by Shuman, Lichtenstein, Claman
Completed 1974

ABINGDON SQUARE PARK

INTERSECTION OF WEST 12TH STREET, 8TH AVENUE AND HUDSON STREET

Abingdon Square Park has a history that extends back to 19th century New York City. Sir Peter Warren, a vice admiral of the British Navy, and his wife Susanna De Lancey, presented a portion of their 300 acres of farmland to their daughter when she got married. That portion is now known as Abingdon Square Park.

In 1831 the Common Council (what is now known as City Council), decided Abingdon Square should be enclosed as a public park and about fifty years later, Parks superintendent Samuel Parsons, Jr. worked with consulting architect Calvert Vaux and redesigned Abingdon Square. In 1921, the Abingdon Square Memorial (aka the Abingdon Doughboy) was dedicated to the local men who fought in World War I. In 1933, a flagstaff was dedicated by the Private Michael J. Lynch Post No. 831 of the Veterans of Foreign Wars.

Designed by Calvert Vaux
Completed 1831

RIVER PLACE BUILDING

© 2014 Mario Burger, Burger International Photography

650 WEST 42ND STREET

River Place is an unlikely space in an unlikely area of town. This section of 42nd Street, a place you would rarely go to on purpose in the '80's, has turned into an up-and-coming neighborhood. This pocket park straddles the River Place building and the Silver Towers to its east. It contains moveable tables and chairs as well as built-in benches, some facing the slide that resemble Adirondack chairs. The slide looks nothing like a slide, however, but more like Pinocchio reclining on the lawn. Built by Tom Otterness, 'Playground' was unveiled in May 2009 and provides a kid-friendly slide for local children who can step on a switch to turn on a sprinkler on hot days. It was placed in the shade to prevent the metal from heating up.

Designed by Thomas Balsley Associates
Completed 2000

MANHATTAN PLAZA

© 2014 Mario Burger, Burger International Photography

448 WEST 43RD STREET

Manhattan Plaza Park is a shady spot on 43rd Street between 9th and 10th Avenues. It has wooden benches, comfortable seating ledges and is accessible on one end by short stairs and on the other by simply walking into the space from the street.

This pocket park was built in 1977 in front of Manhattan Plaza which was originally going to be luxury apartments until the developer went bankrupt. It is now federally-subsidized and became housing for performers and craft workers in the theater industry. When the AIDS crisis hit, it hit the performing arts industry heavily, so many of the residents were affected. Thanks to the late Rev. Rodney Kirk, an Episcopal minister, who established many social services for these residents and for the community at large, the building became a residence primarily for those affected by AIDS who needed assistance in caring for themselves. It is currently a retirement residence for the performing arts community and regularly has a six-year waiting list to rent due to its income scale-based rent plan.

Designed by David Todd & Associates
Completed 1977

ONE WORLDWIDE PLAZA

© 2014 Mario Burger, Burger International Photography

825 EIGHTH AVENUE

Worldwide Plaza, built on one of the former Madison Square Garden sites, is a large plaza that spans 49th and 50th Streets between 8th and 9th Avenues. It contains stationary seating around a large fountain as well as movable tables and chairs scattered throughout the plaza. There are two public restrooms by the 8th Avenue entrance in the arcade. You can enter from 49th or 50th, but the effect is definitely not as dramatic. If you enter from 8th Avenue, and walk through the circular retail arcade, an impressive and unexpected expanse of plaza will open up to you at the end of the corridor.

Worldwide Plaza lends itself to lingering when the weather is nice, but be advised that the management's security guards are adamant about public propriety. They will tell visitors to keep their feet off the chairs and warn sunbathers to keep their shirts on if they dare to take them off. In short, play nice, be respectful to the plaza, and no one will get yelled at.

Designed by SWA Group
Completed 1989

THE SHEFFIELD

322 WEST 57TH STREET

The Sheffield is one of those substantial plazas that extends between West 56th and West 57th. It is more of the 'Concrete Jungle' - type of public space, but the section on West 57th near 9th Avenue hosts a greenmarket. According to a New York greenmarket site, it takes place on Wednesdays and Saturdays and runs year-round. The Sheffield green market has become a neighborhood gathering spot during market days for locals and tourists who are lucky enough, and smart enough, to have ventured away from the usual NYC haunts. Over the years, this space has undergone a couple of renovations and now boasts a lovely gazing pool, built-in seating and a sculpture by David Hostetler called *IKON*. The sculpture was installed on October 17th, 2012.

Designed by Emery Roth & Sons, Thomas Balsley Associates (alterations)
Completed 1978

SAINT LUKE'S - ROOSEVELT HOSPITAL CENTER

1000 10TH AVENUE

This is one of the nicest hospital waiting rooms I have ever seen! The open space on Tenth Avenue between 58th and 59th Streets is accessible through the gate by the drop-off driveway. It features wooden benches, shrubbery and shade trees, and is surrounded by a fence, so look for the gate to enter. There is also usually a food cart located nearby catering to the waiting family members and passersby.

There used to be a crypt holding the remains of James Henry Roosevelt, the founder of Roosevelt Hospital, until the designers agreed it was not a prudent use of space at a hospital where bad things can happen sometimes. The remains were reburied in 1995 in the family crypt at the New York City Marble Cemetery on East 1st Street in the Bowery. A granite monument in his honor remains on the spot.

Designed by Skidmore, Owings & Merrill/Norman Rosenfeld, Buck/Cane
Completed 1990

GENERAL WORTH SQUARE

BROADWAY & 5TH AVENUE & 25TH
STREET

Worth Square is not on the official POPS list, but it is definitely worth a visit. The Worth Monument is the second oldest monument in New York – the oldest being the 1856 George Washington equestrian monument at the southern end of Union Square. Worth Square is located just to the West of Madison Square Park, down in the Flat Iron District and has a number of mobile tables and chairs scattered throughout the space.

Located at the intersection of Broadway, Fifth Avenue, West 24th and West 25th Street, Worth Monument is one of two New York monuments that is also a mausoleum, according to the New York City Parks & Recreation. The other mausoleum is Grant's Tomb in Harlem. Worth Monument is the second oldest monument in New York City after the George Washington monument in Union Square.

Designed by City of New York
Completed 1847

NEW YORK MERCHANDISE MART

41 MADISON AVENUE

New York Merchandise Mart's plaza is in the front of 41 Madison Avenue on the corner of 26th Street. Built on the site of financier Leonard Jerome's mansion, this building was developed to house several industries' showrooms such as manufacturers of gifts and tableware. There are currently 85 different manufacturers on 23 floors.

The seating is without frills, but sometimes you just want a place to stop for a moment when running around Manhattan. The built-in seats with arm-rests are arranged around circular planters. It is out in the open and usual has an interesting push-cart parked nearby if you need a bite to eat or a bottle of water.

Designed by Emery, Roth & Sons
Completed 1972

230 WEST 27TH STREET

© 2014 Mario Burger, Burger International Photography

230 WEST 27TH STREET

In the middle of the FIT (Fashion Institute of Technology) block, and across from the student entrance is a long seating area. It's not easily visible unless you walk under the archway to FIT on Seventh Avenue, but if you go through and look to your left, you will be rewarded. There is a variety of stationary metal benches and planter ledges, but the ledges seem to be discouraged as seating since they are overlaid with sections of stone.

On a recent visit, I saw a guard ask a woman to stop smoking in the space. She moved to the street where outdoor ashtrays were discreetly placed along the curb. It looks as if it is private, but it is indeed accessible to the public at any time. There is also a Starbuck's directly across the street that boasts outdoor seating during more temperate weather.

Designed by de Young & Moscowitz
Completed 1974

CAPITOL PLAZA

58 WEST 26TH STREET

Capitol Plaza is yet another example of Thomas Balsley & Associates' impressive work. This plaza is in an area that is emerging as a residential and creative hub and, until recently, did not have many comfortable public spaces aside from Madison Square Park. The space connects 26th and 27th Street and is just east of 6th Avenue.

A variety of seating options are available from stationary benches to built-in tables with revolving stools, but it's the 90-foot-long orange corrugated metal wall that steals the show. There are bamboo plants behind the wall that peak out through the elliptical cutouts along with a number of shrubs and plantings. As of this date, the original cafe on the 26th Street side has closed, but there is sure to be another one in its place soon. The space begs for one.

Designed by Thomas Balsley & Associates
Completed 2002

HOLIDAY INN EXPRESS

232 WEST 29TH STREET

This space in front of the Holiday Inn Express is actually private property, but does not act like it. When I visited this site, it was filled with tourists off the street looking for a place to have their lunch. It also is not on the City's list of POPS, but is filled with mobile wrought iron tables and chairs, a few benches and is on one of the quieter side streets. With that said, I contacted the hotel to ask if they, indeed, allow the public to use the space. One of their managers said they have no problem with the public using the space as long as a guest is not inconvenienced. She also added that their guests are often out on the town, so the public are the primary visitors of this space.

Designed by unknown
Completed 2006

THE ASCOT

407 PARK AVENUE SOUTH

The Ascot is another example of how I see pocket parks: comfortable spaces parked between two buildings. This one has a gate that is open from morning until dusk and had only wide ledges for seating during my last site visit, but it is tucked back off the street making it a nice place to stop on East 28th Street just east of Park Avenue. It may look as if it is a private, but it is not. Despite the fact that you walk through the space to reach the entrance of the building, the Ascot's pocket park is open to the public.

Look for the sign attached to the drinking fountain: "On this site in 1897 nothing happened."

Designed by Thomas Balsley Associates
Completed 1984

ONE PENN PLAZA

1 PENNSYLVANIA PLAZA

Bordered by Seventh Avenue, West 33rd, 8th Avenue and West 34th, One Penn Plaza is a massive space. Some of it is simple ledge seating on its own or around a planting, some mobile tables and chairs, and then there is the space out back by 8th Avenue between 33rd and 34th Streets. Here you will find a pass-through type of space along with various seating heights, tables, a restaurant and a few food kiosks to go along with the usual push carts you find near Penn Station. If you need a rest room, you can buy a cup of coffee and duck into one of the usual coffee bars.

Designed by Kahn and Jacobs; Thomas Balsley Associates (renovations)
Completed 1972

WORLD APPAREL CENTER

1411 BROADWAY

The World Apparel Center is located in the center of the Fashion District and is bordered by Broadway and 7th Avenue and 39th and 40th Streets. This building was created as a place to house various clothing manufacturers and actually has two spaces where tourists and sit. One on the corner of Broadway and 39th is more a series of stairs, the center of which is the home of a bronze bust of Golda Meir created by the sculptor Beatrice Goldfine. If you head west to the corner of 7th Avenue and 39th, you will find a sculpture of a man at a sewing machine titled *The Garment Worker.* It represents the immigrants who came to New York as garment workers and provided a source of cheap labor for the industry. Next to that is the Garment District's information center. Its whimsical design is a giant needle and a button appropriately titled *Needle Threading a Button.* There are often moveable tables and chairs near the 7th Avenue location.

Designed by Irwin Chanin
Completed 1968

PHILIP MORRIS

© 2014 Mario Burger, Burger International Photography

120 PARK AVENUE

This is one of the first pocket parks or public spaces I remember. I was new to New York City and an old friend bought me there to eat our lunch (take-out from Zaro's). Its four-story indoor space has mobile seating, built-in benches and displays sculptures from the permanent collection of the Whitney Museum of American Art.

The Philip Morris Atrium is located on the southwest corner of Park Avenue and 42nd Street, just across the street from Grand Central Terminal. The entry from the Park Avenue side, however, is the most rewarding as it gives you a view of the entire space from several steps above it all. I have also heard there is a public restroom available, but you have to obtain a key from the guard. For what it's worth, I have personally never been aware of a restroom. Perhaps it is a well-kept secret!

Designed by Ulrich Franzen
Completed 1982

1185 SIXTH AVENUE

1185 SIXTH AVENUE

1185 Sixth Avenue runs between 46th and 47th Streets just west of Sixth. It used to be called the Westpoint Stevens Tower, but is currently listed as the Stevens Tower in the New York City Department of City Planning's POPS database. Whatever its name, it is a large pass-through space just west of 6th Avenue between 46th and 47th Streets. One of its more prominent features is its built-in ledge seating around large planters and as part of the adjacent building along with a fountain. A nearby theatre housing up to 400 seats is accessed from the plaza and an outdoor cafe makes use of the moveable seating available to the public. A neat feature is the restaurant overhead that connects the two buildings.

Designed by Emery Roth & Sons
Completed 1970

1211 AVENUE OF THE AMERICAS

© 2014 Nicholas Alfonso

1211 SIXTH AVENUE

Known as the News Corp Building, this is not a lush space, but more of a platform on the southwest corner of Sixth Avenue and 48th Street. It is actually part of a larger through block arcade which is part of the Rockefeller Center area that extends through the building to the west. The plaza contains four built-in benches of which the Avenue-side is popular as a place to people watch. The space is surrounded by trees that are about the only lush part of the plaza, but it is a good place to get some sun during a break and the trees soften the feeling of concrete. The 48th Street side also has an entrance to the Rockefeller Center subway station serving the B-D-F-M lines.

Designed by Harrison and Abramovitz
Completed 1973

1166 SIXTH AVENUE

1166 6TH AVENUE

1166 Sixth Avenue passes between 45th & 46th Streets. The neighborhood known as Little Brazil flanks it on the 46th Street side between Fifth and Sixth Avenues.

This park is peaceful and one of those comfortable, well-planned parks with many levels. Both built-in benches and moveable tables and chairs are scattered throughout the space, and there are a number of plantings and trees throughout. On the 45th Street side, there is a sculpture that seems to floating in the pool of the fountain. *Throwback (1976-1979)* is an abstract sculpture made from black aluminum and created by Tony Smith. The 46th Street side features a Memorial to the souls from March & McLennan who were lost on 9/11. The inscription can be found at http://memorial.mmc.com/. 7/16/2003

Designed by Skidmore, Owings & Merrill
Completed 1972
Note: Alterations by Sasaki Associates (1981), Kliment & Halsband (1989)

575 FIFTH AVENUE

575 FIFTH AVENUE

The headquarters of L'Oreal at 575 Fifth Avenue is one of those spaces I may have discounted had I not seen it in person for myself. The outside is deceptive, looking like the usual entrance to a department store. When you enter on 47th Street, however, you discover a large space that ascends four stories high. The first level is a well-lit space throughout which moveable tables and chairs are scattered around a small fountain. Public restrooms are located on the main and second floors, a welcome amenity for those of us who visit, but do not live in or have an office, the city. 575 Fifth Avenue is an excellent place to stop if you need a rest or have to use the restroom, and a great place to duck into on a rainy or snowy day.

Designed by Emery Roth & Sons
Completed 1983

MCGRAW-HILL

137 WEST 48TH STREET

Located at the 48th Street side of the space, this waterfall behind the McGraw-Hill Building is different than the waterfall in other parks because you walk through it by way of a tube set into the waterfall. This is one of the quintessential vest pocket parks because it sits between buildings and provides a little extra ambience by the introduction of the waterfall and its interesting design. The space extends between 48th and 49th Street just west of Sixth Avenue. As you head toward 49th Street, you come upon moveable tables and chairs which visitors often pull close to the west wall to escape the blazing sun. If you were to visit just one of the parks in this guide, this would be one I would suggest you put high on your list.

Designed by Harrison & Abramovitz & Harris
Completed 1971

745 SEVENTH AVENUE

745 7TH AVENUE

Across from the McGraw-Hill park with the tube waterfall is 745 Seventh Avenue. This, too, is located just west of Seventh Avenue between 49th Street and 50th Streets. Slightly larger than its counterpart across the street, 745 Seventh Avenue becomes wider toward the 50th Street entrance. The space features a number of moveable tables and chairs, some polished wood built-in benches, and a fountain on the Eastern wall.

Designed by Kohn Pedersen Fox Associates
Completed 2001

NEW YORK PALACE HOTEL

457 MADISON AVENUE

The New York Palace Hotel is part of the New York Palace Hotel and the oldest POPS in the city according to Jerold S. Kayden. Formerly the Villard Mansion, built for financier Henry Villard, it is a popular place for movie shoots, weddings and fundraising events due to its opulent decor. It is also located directly across the street from the back of Saint Patrick Cathedral. When I discovered it, there were two men in kilts next to a stunning lady in a satin dress waiting for a wedding photographer. Movable tables and chairs and intricate Florentine lanterns are scattered around courtyard which is open to the public unless reserved for an event.

Designed by MkKim, Mead & White; Emery Roth & Sons
Completed 1978

SEAGRAM'S PLAZA

375 PARK AVENUE

Located on Park Avenue between 52nd and 53rd Street, Seagram's Plaza inspired the city to pass a resolution for more public space in 1961. While the resolution was not completely successful in that the spaces are not properly monitored for compliance, it did lead to many amazing outdoor plazas and pocket parks throughout New York City.

It was built during a time when accessibility was not a major concern for builders. As such, the plaza, as well as the two side entrances, are raised from the sidewalk by several steps which makes it difficult to enjoy if you are in a wheelchair or encumbered by a walker, for example. With that said, it is a nice place to catch some rays and people-watch if it is not too hot outside. If it is, the sun has a tendency to beat down on this space.

Designed by Ludwig Mies van der Rohe
Completed 1960

LEVER HOUSE

390 PARK AVENUE

Though the Seagram's Building across the street is widely credited with the beginning of the city's love of urban plazas, Lever House was the actual pioneer. The developers wanted to illustrate Lever Bros. identity as a soap company by creating a "squeaky clean" design. The result was to sacrifice valuable ground-floor real estate in exchange for wide-open public space under the building at street level.

The plaza to the south past the glass-enclosed elevator banks is where the seating is located. The building takes up the entire block and is a nice spot to take a break if you are looking for some shade. Head to the southern side by 53rd Street. That's where the scant greenery as well as a seating can be found.

Designed by Skidmore, Owings and Merrill
Completed 1951

CONTINENTAL ILLINOIS BUILDING

520 MADISON AVENUE

The Continental Illinois Building's plaza entered on 53rd Street just west of Madison Avenue feeds my sense of wonder. It's stuffed between two buildings, contains moveable chairs and tables, a ledge on which to sit, and it is open to the public. The thing that makes it cool, other than the waterfall sliding down the side of one of its bordering buildings, is that it contains a piece of the Berlin Wall.

According to Ephemeral New York, Jerry Speyer of Tishman Speyer (owner of the plaza) purchased the piece from the East German government and had it installed in 1990. It is there for the public to enjoy. You can grab a coffee, sit down and enjoy a bit of world history, and a bit of peace, courtesy of Tishman Speyer.

Designed by Swanke Hayden Connell
Completed 1982

CHRISTIE'S GARDEN

© 2014 Mario Burger, Burger International Photography

535 MADISON AVENUE

Christie's Garden, located at 535 Madison Avenue at the northeast corner of 54th Street, is interesting due to the cut-away at the bottom of the building in which it sits. When you look at it, it seems impossible that the building can stay up with just the column that supports that corner. The lobby of Christie's Auction House is enclosed in glass, so it looks out onto the plaza filled with greenery, flowering trees and a waterfall. Christie's provides rotating exhibits from their collection of sculptures. Movable tables and chairs are scattered throughout the plaza and the gentle sounds of water as it passes over the waterfall provides a nice backdrop to the sounds of the city.

Designed by Edward Larrabee Barnes
Completed 1982

IBM HEADQUARTERS ATRIUM

590 MADISON AVENUE

The IBM Atrium is one of those places that can take your breath away. Enter on the 56th Street side just west of Madison Avenue and you will be treated to a four-story atrium enclosed primarily in glass. Scattered throughout the space are groupings of bamboo in planters inserted directly into the granite floor and moveable tables and chairs take advantage of the filtered sunlight. There are permanent food kiosks, rotating modern art exhibits and 'Levitated Mass,' a granite horizontal fountain created by Michael Heizer. The fountain is located at the Madison Avenue entrance.

Designed by architect Edward Larrabee Barnes and landscape architect Robert Zion
Completed 1982 (1994 alteration by Robert A. M. Stern)

GRAND CENTRAL PLAZA

622 THIRD AVENUE

Grand Central Plaza is on top of a building only two stories tall, carefully nestled above crowded Third Avenue. It provides a rare bit of peace and quiet in the middle of NYC. If the 41 stairs are too daunting for you, there is an elevator located on the left after you walk under the clock.

At the top of the stairs, the space opens up providing views of the surrounding buildings. It's like sitting in a nest in a treetop if trees had seats or people sat in nests. Benches line the walls and stationary tables and chairs along with a few movable chairs are scattered throughout the space.

Designed by Emery Roth & Sons; Moed de Armas & Shannon/Thomas Balsley Associates (for alterations)
Completed 1971

TUDOR CITY GREENS

42ND STREET AND FIRST AVENUE

Tudor City Greens is an elevated park that straddles 42nd Street at the East end of 42nd by First Avenue. Fred F. French, a real estate developer, saw the need for a tranquil residential area for busy middle class New Yorkers and began building Tudor City in 1927. As a result, Tudor City was built around parks and open spaces.

After French died in 1936, his firm owned and managed the Tudor City buildings until the property was purchased by the Helmsley-Spears Company in 1972 and Time Equities, Inc., in 1987. Time Equities, Inc. donated it to The Trust for Public Land putting an end to future development and construction in the parks. Tudor City Greens, Inc., formed in 1987, is currently tasked with the upkeep and preservation of the parks.

Designed by Fred French and H. Douglas Ives
Completed 1928

JAMES P. GRANT PLAZA

301 EAST 44TH STREET

James P. Grant Plaza, located between First and Second Avenues, was dedicated in June of 1996 as part of UNICEF's 50th anniversary celebration. It honors the former Executive Director of UNICEF who worked tirelessly to combat preventable childhood illness and launched a 'child survival and development revolution' in 1983 that save the lives of an estimated 12 million children.

The park contains a number of benches surrounding trees and plantings as well as the *Spirit of Audrey* sculpture which was unveiled on May 7, 2002, to honor Audrey Hepburn's work also on behalf of the world's children. In 2003, the park was turned into a temporary post office complete with a special envelope to commemorate the unveiling.

Designed by Kevin Roche John Dinkeloo and Associates
Completed 1987 (Re-dedicated 1996)

DAG HAMMARSKJOLD PLAZA

866 SECOND AVENUE

In 1997, this large plaza located at East 47th Street between First and Second Avenues underwent a $2.3 million reconstruction complete with park benches, better lighting, a steel lattice dome and the Katharine Hepburn Garden. Dag Hammarskjold was a scholar from Sweden who held a number of governmental positions including Secretary-General of the United Nations. Dag Hammarskjold Plaza was dedicated in 1961 after his death in a plane crash en route to a diplomatic mission in the Congo.

Dedicated in 1997, the Katherine Hepburn Garden, located closer to Second Avenue, is a tribute to Ms. Hepburn's love of flowers and her work to maintain the esthetics of Turtle Bay.

Designed by George Vellonakis
Completed 1997

601 LEXINGTON AVENUE

153 EAST 53RD STREET

Formerly known as the Atrium at Citigroup Center, this public space located on Lexington Avenue by 53rd Street is an impressive indoor and outdoor public space. Inside there are three stories of restaurants and shops, movable tables and chairs, and public restrooms. Outside resembles a sunken living room with stairs heading down from street level and a fountain with water cascading over stones. The Atrium is usually busy, both indoors and outside, and includes an entrance to the subway.

Designed by Gwathmey Siegel & Associates
Completed 1975

BRIDGEMARKET PLAZA

409 EAST 59TH STREET

The Evangeline Blashfield Fountain is one of those illustrations of the frequent benevolence of New Yorkers. Dedicated in May 1919 in honor of a patron of public space in New York City, the Evangeline Blashfield Fountain was built to provide water for the vendors at the open-air market that originally stood on the site. In 2002, various patrons and economic agencies combined to restore it to its original beauty.

It sits at the end of the plaza beneath the 59th Street Bridge. When the hall is not engaged, the plaza is open to the public. Often loud due to bridge traffic, it is worth a trip to visit this testimony to a benevolent person and the magnificent detail in this mosaic.

Designed by Olin Partnership
Completed 2002

DAVID RUBENSTEIN ATRIUM

61 WEST 62ND STREET

The David Rubenstein Atrium, formerly known as the Harmony Atrium, was renovated and renamed in 2009 after Rubenstein's generous $10 million gift to the Bravo Campaign. This lively indoor public space located on Broadway between 62nd and 63rd Streets is a welcome respite especially on days when the weather is not cooperating. It contains benches and movable tables and chairs, Chef Tom Colicchio's 'wichcraft café, free wifi, a restroom (a very helpful amenity indeed), or free weekly performances of anything from a big band performance to a poetry slam. All of this takes place next to two vertical gardens, a media wall available for video presentations, and an art installation by Dutch textile artisan Claudy Jongstra. The Atrium is open various hours from 8am to 10pm depending on the day of the week.

Designed by Tod Williams Billie Tsien Architects
Completed 2009

1886 BROADWAY/30 LINCOLN PLAZA

1186 BROADWAY/30 LINCOLN PLAZA

This space is directly behind Lincoln Plaza Cinema which faces Broadway between 62nd and 63rd Streets. The most dramatic entrance is on 63rd Street just east of Broadway. As you come upon the space, you find an impressive park-like space with movable chairs, stationary benches and a beautiful waterfall in the center.

Much of the space is taken up by brickwork and the landscaping by the waterfall, but it is still a lovely space to visit. The sound of the waterfall is soothing and the greenery makes it feel as if you are in nearby Central Park albeit with more buildings.

Designed by M. Paul Friedberg
Completed 1978

WEST END TOWERS

75 WEST END AVENUE

This large park on West End Avenue between 63rd and 64th Street overseen by West End Towers across the street to the south. With lots of shade trees and built-in benches surrounding a playground, this park is a lovely place to stop even without your kids. The western half of the park is a series of paths around plantings and hosts a sculpture of a rhino on his nose called *Newton and Darwin* by sculptor Nobi Shioya. The sculpture is located near the 64th Street side between the playground and the path area. Look for the inscription at the base of the sculpture.

Designed by Quennell Rothschild Associates
Completed 1993

TRAMWAY PLAZA

EAST 60TH STREET AND 2ND AVENUE

Tramway Plaza sits just beneath the entrance to the Roosevelt Island Tramway, a tram built in 1976 that takes commuters between Manhattan and Roosevelt Island to the east. This is a comfortable space filled with several built-in benches and mature trees and plantings. Installed in 2013, *Hosea*, a 15-foot tall sculpture created by Carole Eisner from a railroad gear is and impressive feature located directly in the center of the space.

Designed by New York City of Parks and Recreation
Completed 1980

211 EAST 70TH STREET

© 2014 Mario Burger, Burger International Photography

211 EAST 70TH STREET

Just east of Third Avenue is a secluded, gated park open to the public despite its classification as private space. Its gates have not been closed during any of my site visits. The space is a pass-through between 70th and 71st Streets and is overrun (in a good way) by ivy, various trees and plantings. Nestled amidst all of this are several built-in benches and ledges on which to sit.

With its walls and high fences, this is a place to go if you want a little distance between the bustling city streets, but a bit too secluded to visit at night.

Designed by Emery Roth & Sons
Completed 1975

ONE EAST RIVER PLACE

525 EAST 72ND STREET

This is a lovely, shady park at the extreme east end of 72nd Street east of York Street. It is filled with movable tables and chairs, built-in benches, several mature trees and a soothing waterfall toward the back. The trees are lit at night and the guard in the gatehouse just outside by the street lends a feeling of relative safety. With all of these amenities, it is a favorite lunchtime hangout for workers from the nearby offices and apartment dwellers alike. If you head farther east, just a few steps away, you will be treated to a view of the East River along with several benches on which to sit and enjoy the view of the river as well as the dogs who visit this area for their daily walk.

Designed by Davis, Brody & Associates
Completed 1988

CONTINENTAL TOWERS

301 EAST 79TH STREET

The elevated space directly to the east of Second Avenue on the north side of 79th Street contains stationary tables and chairs and several large potted trees. It was originally supposed to be extended back toward 80th Street as a park-like plaza, but that never happened. It can get very sunny and hot in the warmer months. With that said, it is a calm, quiet place to stop due to its slight elevation by way of a few steps which acts as a buffer to nearby traffic and city sounds.

Designed by M. Paul Friedberg
Completed 1977

ABOUT THE AUTHOR

First in a series of guides celebrating the nation's littlest green spaces, *Best Pocket Parks of NYC* began when Rosemary O'Brien found herself between acting auditions and seeking quiet in a busy city. Tracking down – and enjoying – dozens of New York City pocket parks inspired this compilation of her best finds.

Rosemary O'Brien is a website content producer, educator and published author of two novels, *First Saturday* and *Scraps*. She is among writers featured in Dallas Hodder Franklin's *Dare to be Published! 50 Authors Help You Write, Market & Publish in the New Century.*

Her work with the Entrepreneurship Boot Camp for Veterans' Families (EBV-F) led O'Brien to grow *Best Pocket Parks of NYC* from one book to a publishing venture. A wife and mother, she holds a degree in creative writing and lives with her family in Connecticut.

7/16/14

CPSIA information can be obtained at www.ICGtesting.com
Printed in the USA
LVOW06s1556120314

377119LV00009BA/229/P

Oc